In the shopp

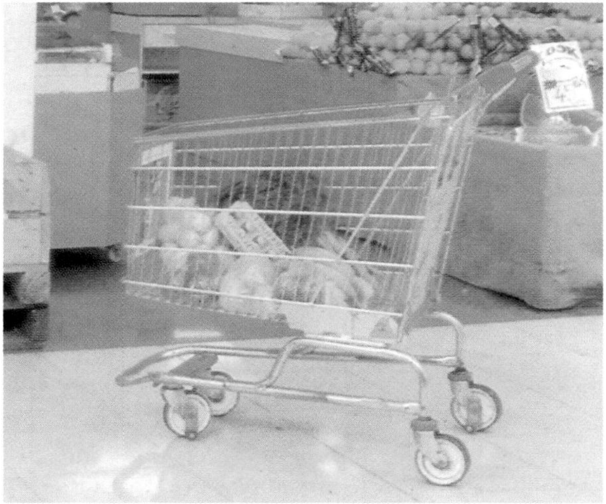

We like bananas.

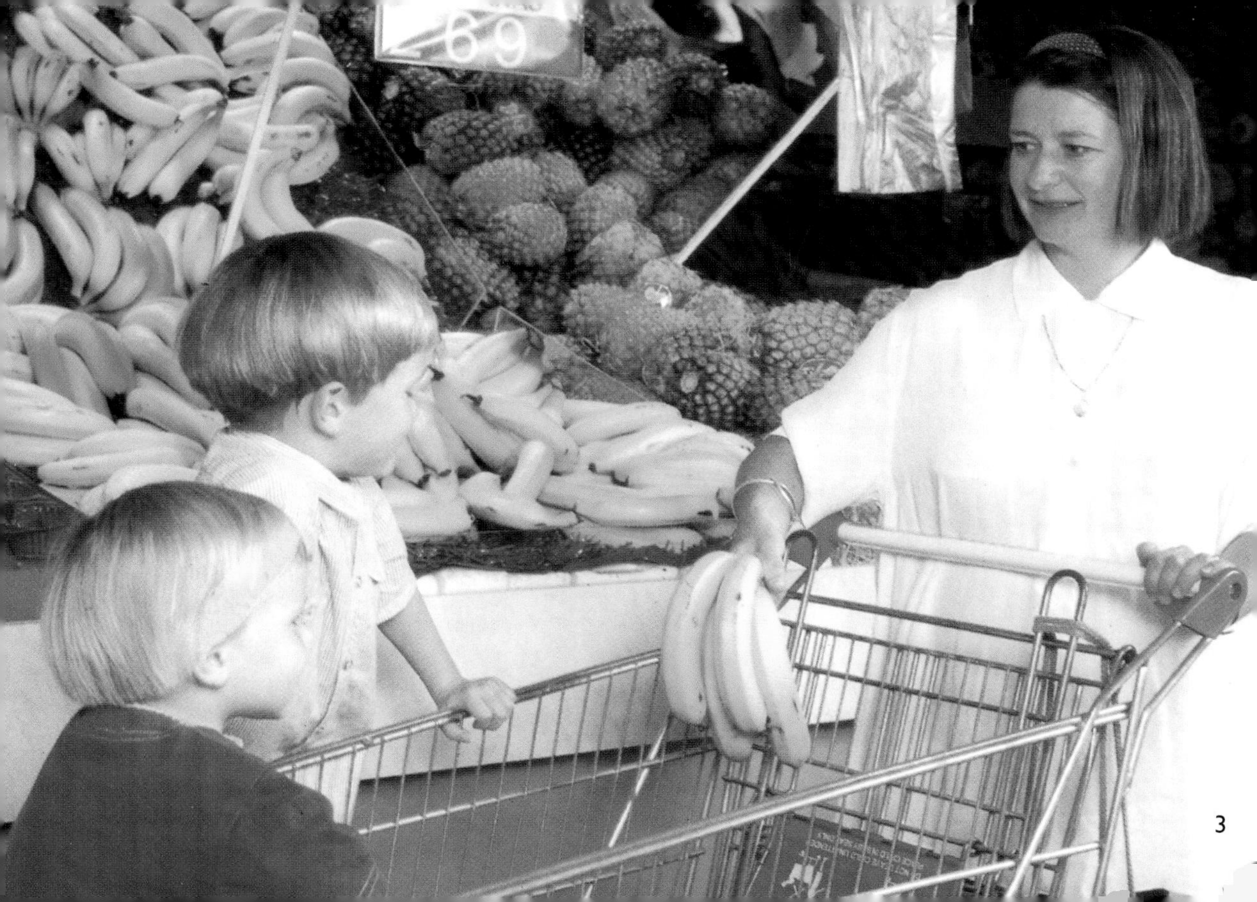

We like apples.

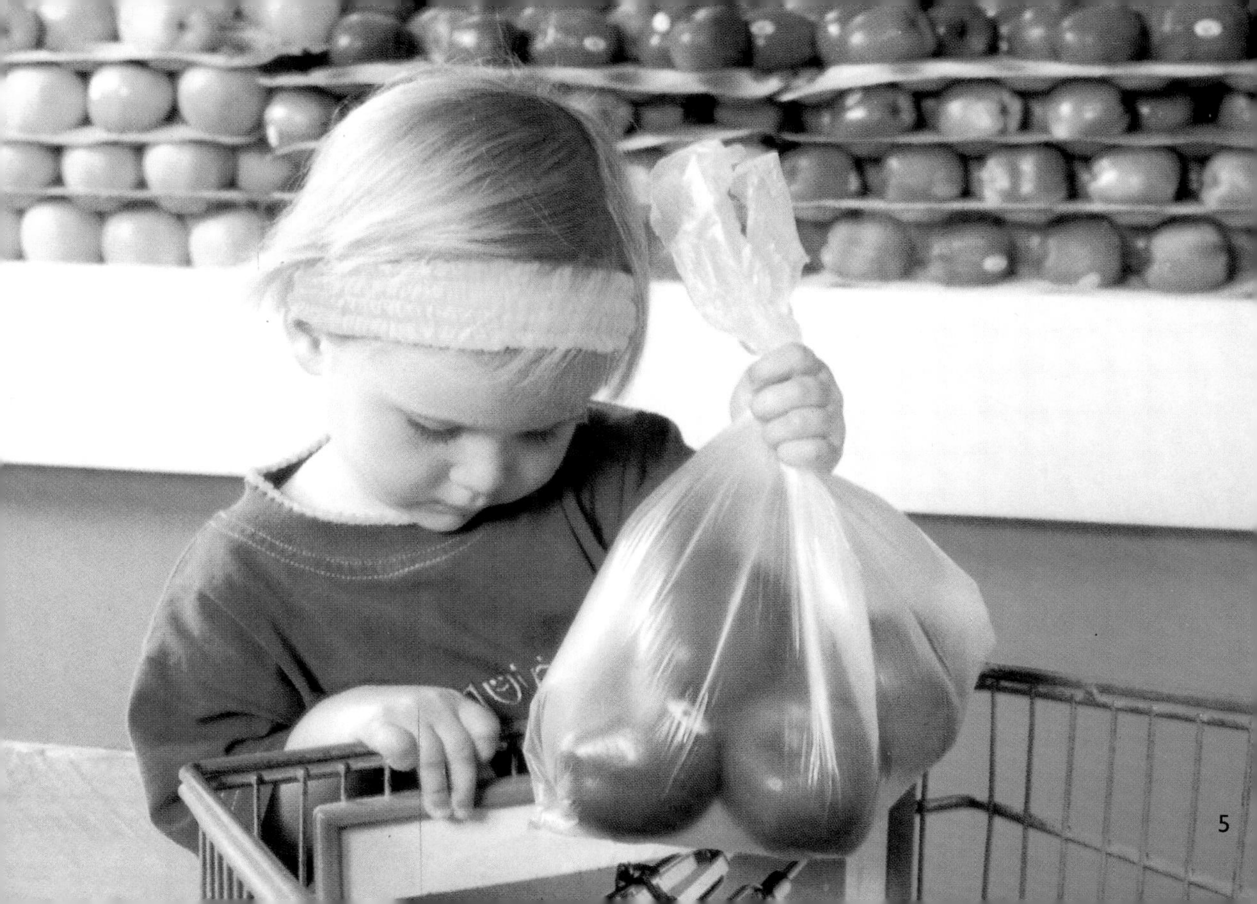

We like oranges.

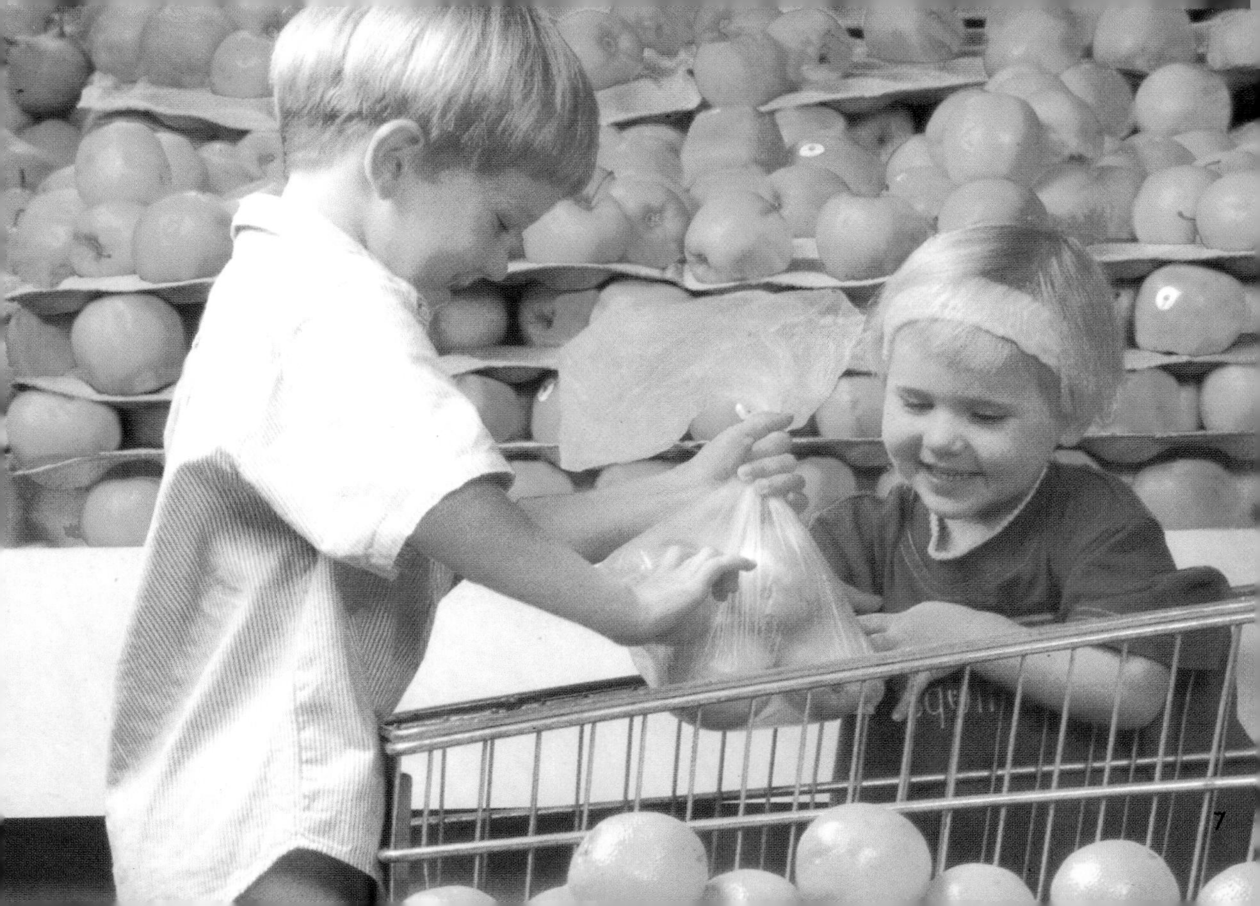

We like tomatoes.

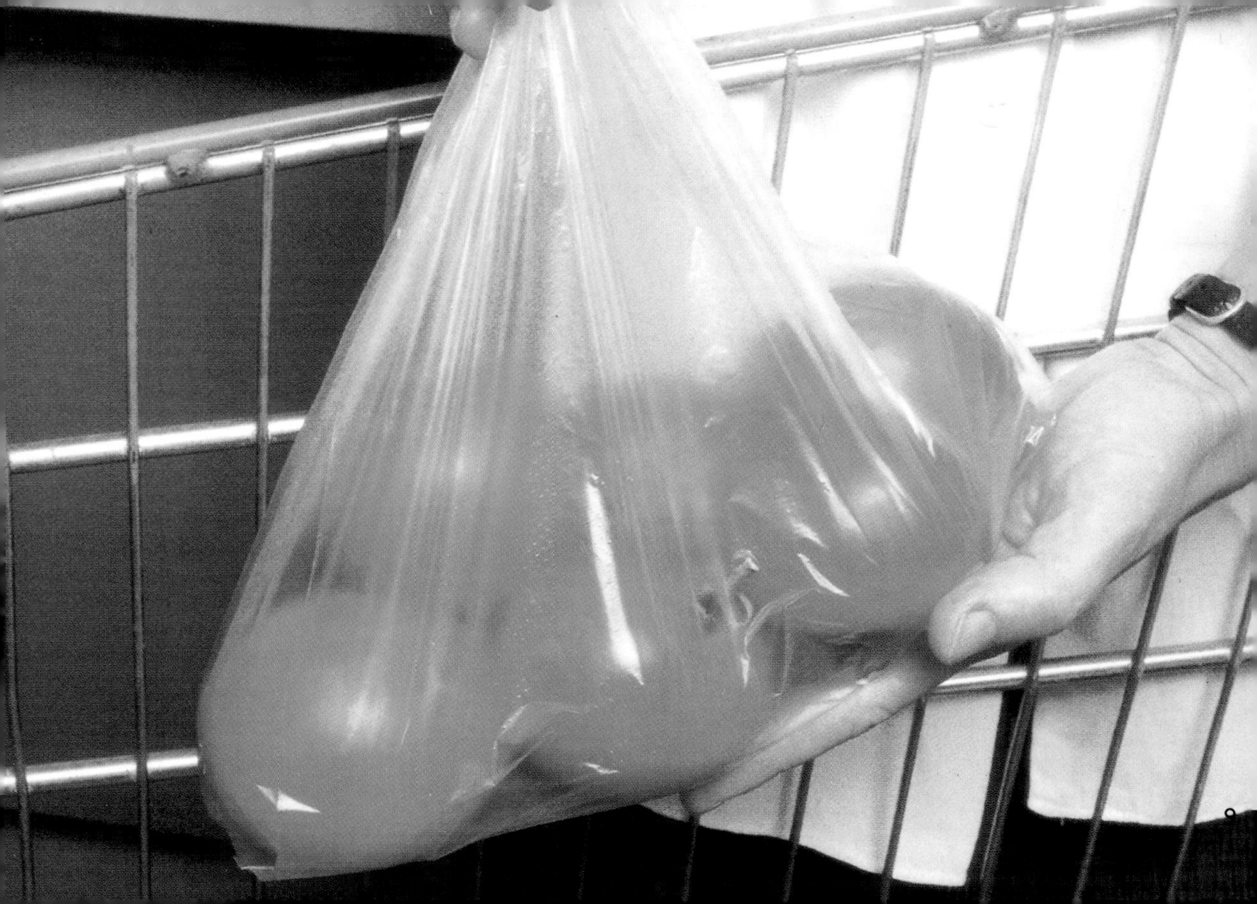

We like carrots.

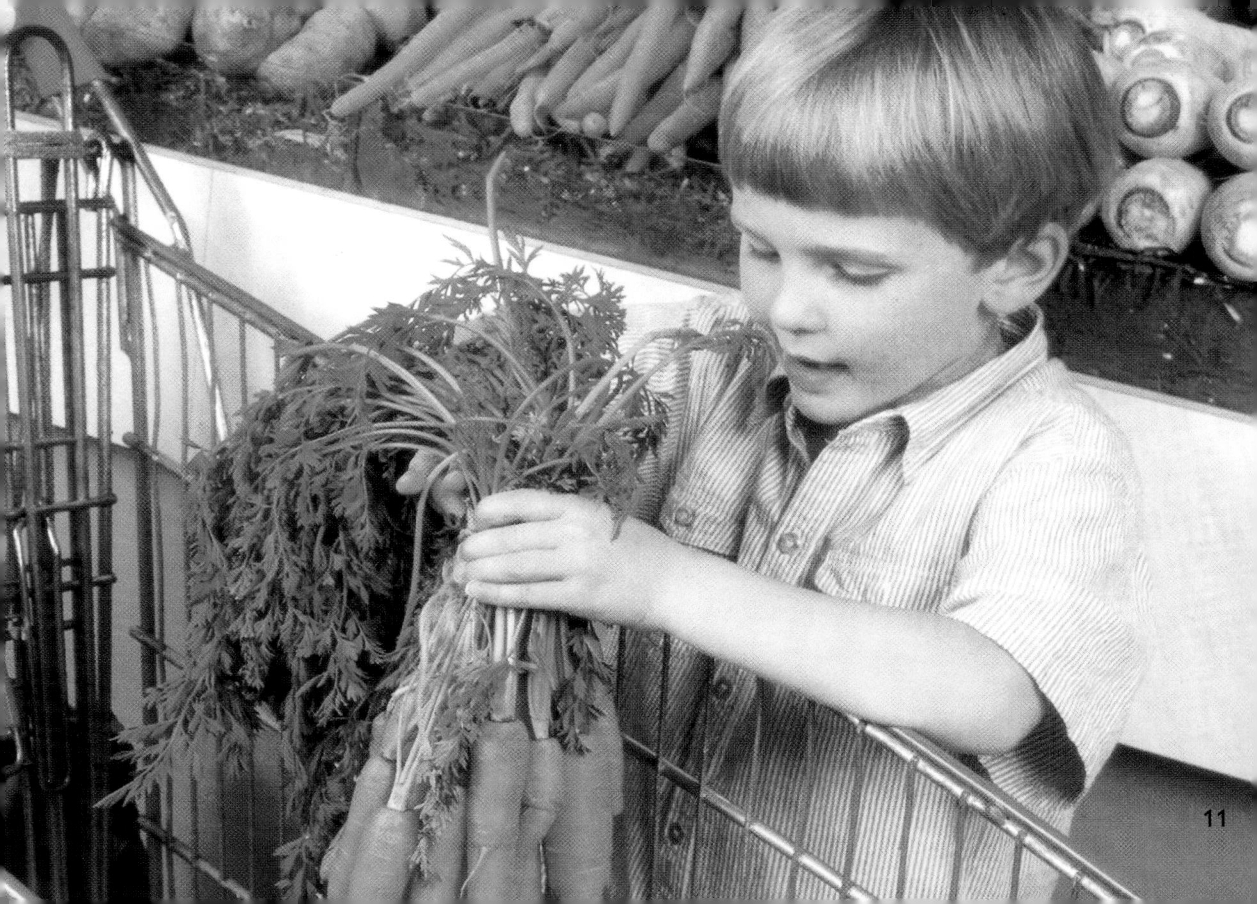

We like potatoes.

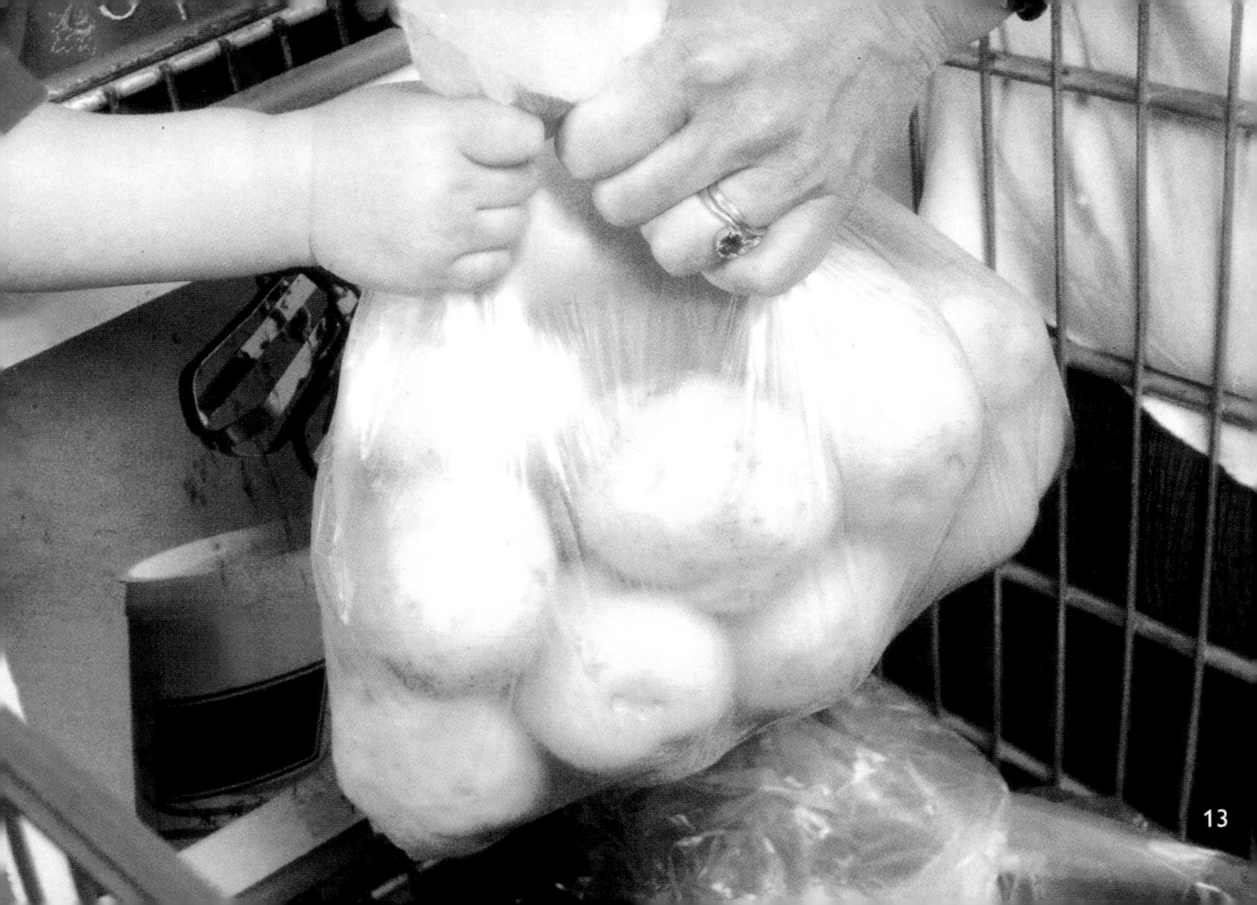

We like eggs.

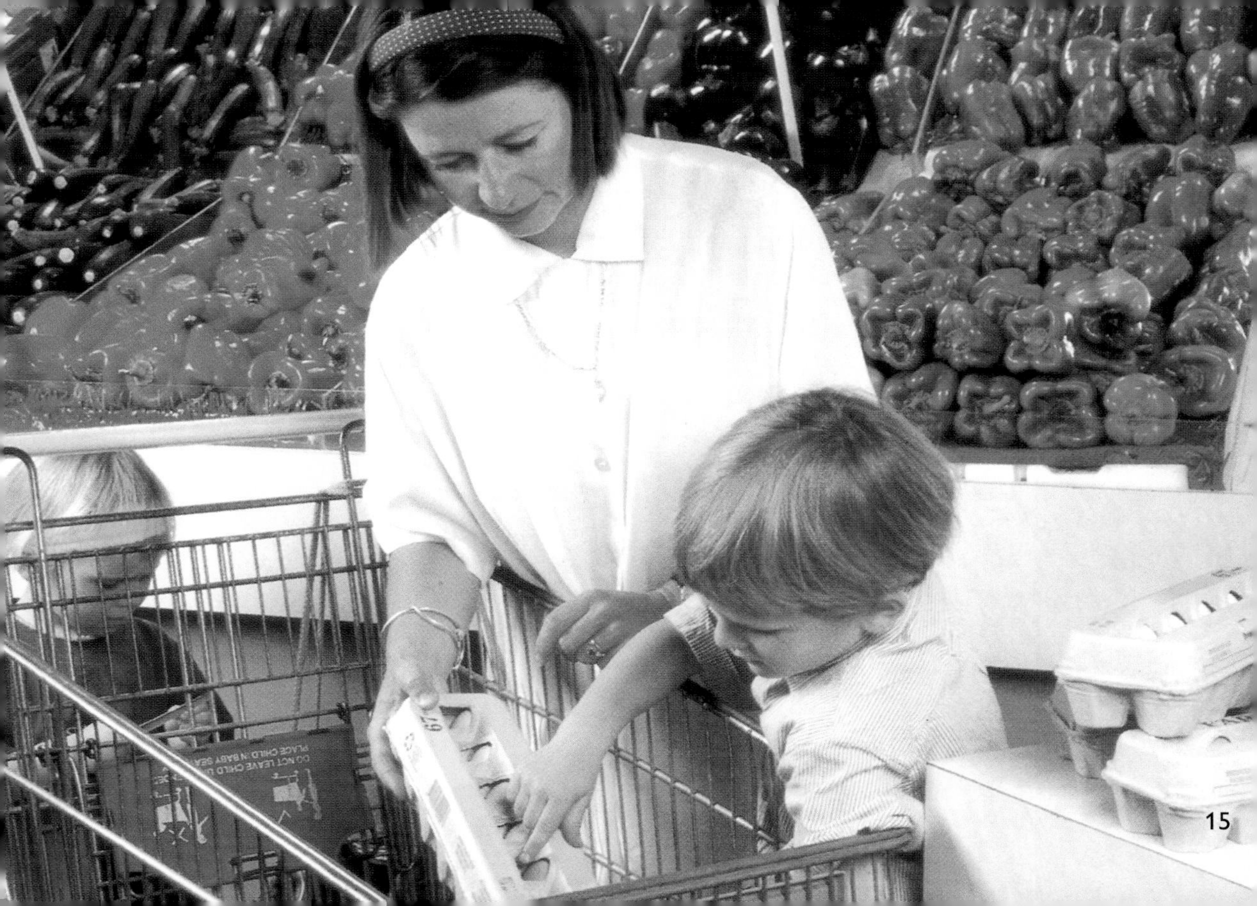

We like everything!

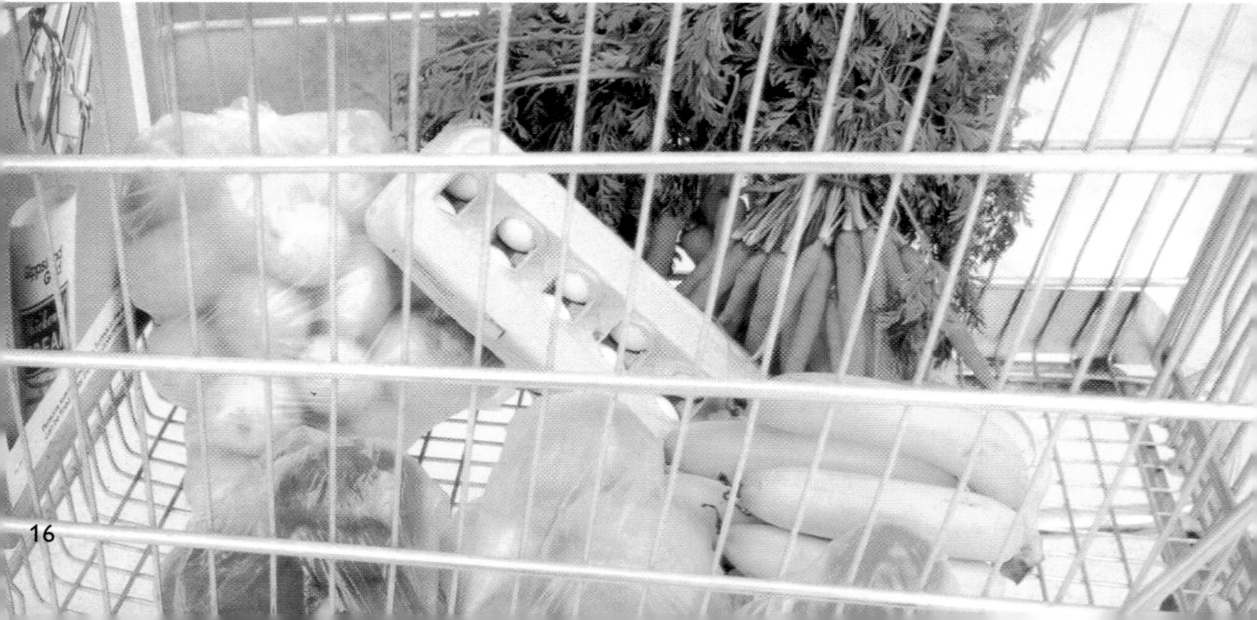